I am a child

NOT an Adult

Published September 2025

1st Edition

Contents

We are living in a time when critical race theory in the form of anti-black racism awareness, is being cancelled.

Such that projects that centered equity through literature and arts for black people, in many places are being banned.

While this is not banned, here are some reflections...on Adultification

Most of this text is written from the **point of view of a child**.

Poem - Still A Child

Please don't call him the bad one

He's high energy and young
He has reems of enthusiasm

True, he can be hard to control
That's his role as a child soul

Please don't keep calling him naughty
He's still forming oracy. He's five not forty

He can be excited confused less regulated
Note he could be SEND, black and tropically segregated

Please don't say he's the bad one
Instead consider he is someone's son

He maybe taxing to your methods and mental energy
It takes a village to manage children with this much vitality

Just don't say he's the one to scrutinise
He just expressing connections, see he tries

Just take a moment and see, keep calm
Amongst his expressing is a kind of kiddie charm

Just don't say he is the one to specially watch

Unless you want to celebrate him having fun playing
hopscotch

He doesn't need a bad label he's only five
So, if he fidgets that's just a sign of being alive

23rd April 2025

A polite request:

Please don't be offended by these writings.

It may or may not apply to you.

If it does not fully apply to you, still read it

and

pass it on so it will help future adults and children

The child Monologue begins:

I am a child

and I want to learn from kind,

respectful adults,

who can treat me as

a great child

who can grow into a great adult

I am a human too, like you, and the people you love and care about

I am not the same as a character

from the television, social media, a cartoon, a music videos, a song lyric, a newspaper story,

a folk-tale, a movie, or advertisement.

I am just

me.

And that is great.

I am not a symbol of your past relationship with

Your daughter, son,

partner, ex-friend, ex-partner, father, mother,

grandparent,

or anyone else

I am a 21st century child – a human 2.0.

I am ready to be healthier and happier

than

humans before

because of this

modern world

has much to

share

I am

    a child.

    just me, unique,

    not the same as anyone you

    knew, know and will do so in the future.

        I'm unique at this moment in time

If I don't respond to you the way you expect,

...

it can be because

I am a child, and I process like a child,

I might be tired, overwhelmed, dreamy,

...

I am just human

and young

If I lose focus,

it is because I am ... a child

If I chat ... it is because ...

I want to be heard

If I don't do the work ... it's because ...

I am human and

sometimes, I am not inspired

by what other people want me to do

sometimes I think of something else

Sometimes I am tired of the work given to me

Sometimes I do not enjoy *the work*

there are many kinds of ...sometimes

...

Am I allowed to not like the work and not do it - please?

When I am distressed ...

> please don't coerce me with an aggressive tone

Please don't tell me my future depends on me doing this task

Please don't communicate with me with anger towards me in your mind

Please don't communicate to me with

passive aggressive body language

Please don't reward me with junk food

Please don't tug me in any way if you are annoyed

Please don't let me feel like you dislike me

Please don't be cold to me

I am a ... child

When you are in the role of guardian over me

...

please don't have negative
thoughts towards me

If I fidget ...

It is because I am a mammal and mammals need to move

I am a human not a robot

I am a human not a statue

I am a living moving being

Please don't take away my fidget toy ...

it does provide me with comfort in

this busy overwhelming world for
a child like me

If I walk wobbly ...

It might be because it feels nice...

I am not doing it to offend you

Please don't punish me by missing my break time.

Playtime is how I let off steam from being stationery in a classroom for several hours

Please don't think the carrot and stick way of behaving towards me is the only method to educate me, I do like autonomy like Montessori

Mostly, I don't want to come in from the short playtime. I enjoy it more than some of the lessons.

I want to enjoy my life

I want to enjoy my time

I want to enjoy being in school

If my uniform looks dirty, and my hygiene is poor, ...

please be an advocate for my well being

Sometimes .., I love to laugh loudly

If I talk to another child ...

It might be because I love to speak

to young people my age

If I don't sit still ...

It might be because I feel happy when I move

Quote from a 6-year-old boy	Quote from a 8-year-old boy
I am tired, I just want to go home and play with my toy	But I don't understand how to do that math's
Quote from a 7-year-old boy	**Quote from a 9-year-old girl**
I don't know how to read yet, I have not been taught.	Are you Nigerian. I am Nigerian. You look like me.

If I talk loudly ...

It might be because I have vocal cords that like to be exercised, just like how my legs are exercised

If I am whispering,

It might be because

I have a thought, and I

wanted to get it out

Please don't be in the habit of restraining me,

with tight my body to your body locks or pinning my arms behind my back to frog march me, or

be standing over me with the threat of being restrained for not moving at your request

Please remember not matter what is on my report, or what people say about me, **I am a child** with a future, but still a child in mind, body and emotion.

Please know if I have any traumas,

(not to pity me)

to know if I am easily triggered and

know how to **prevent my buttons being pressed** as I grow through this period

Please know if I am triggered around you

Please know how to keep me calm

Please don't treat me as any kind of negative label

Adultification is different for every adultified child

What is adultification?

It is treating a child like me as an adult like you.

Not considering my developmental stage.

It is racial.

What can adultification look like?

Behaviour	White child	Brown Asian/Black Child
Late for school	Sympathy ←→	Anger
Messy work Work averse	Support ←→	Impatience
Poor behaviour	Speak to parents ←→	Detention
		Restrain

Dear Adults,

With self-awareness,

it is easy to switch and be the nice version

History and Adultification

Adultification comes from colonial history.

Here's how...

English is my language by force in history

English is my second language

English is not my indigenous language

English is not spoken at home

English is new to some generations in my family

English culture is something I am learning every day

Letters

Dear Adult,

If I don't sound articulate, like Berty or Arthur or Roger or Gerald or Mattias or Tilly or Lilliana or Emily or Anouska it may be because they have benefited from an uninterrupted uncolonized history.

For several hundred years, my ancestral language, land and culture were oppressed by European powers

Right now, I am catching up with my European classmates. Equity helps me to catch up.

Dear Adult,

If I do sound angry, can you be patient and see me as just human, nice, kind and squidgy.

Please rid any negative racial tropes from you mind and actions

Dear Adult,

A polite reminder:

Please don't be afraid of me, the depth of my colour, my facial features, my hair structure, my feet and hands, or the perceived thickness of my bones

Please don't fetish anyway I may be physically different to the white people you know

Dear Adult,

Please think of me as a prince or princess, warranting respect and consideration.

I just want to expand my mind.

I just want to live in happiness, in peace and joy

I am still young

Dear Adult,

If you notice any of my strengths, please encourage and help me to develop them

Dear Adult,

If I do anything you think is rude, please be warm and patient with me while I learn better

Dear Adult,

Please don't shrug off or go along with **ignoring my distress**, if that is the culture around me.

Please don't let me be separated from the class by any barrier.

Please interrupt if people start thinking of me as the bad one.

Please be a brave advocate for me.

I can do something bad, but it doesn't make me a bad person.

Culture and society effects all of us...

Everyone is defined in society, generally those more favoured are those European / light skinned / straight haired, narrow featured ... all because of colonial history.

It's a history that divided the world, in hierarchies of skin tones and race.

It's a lie.

We are all beautiful, old or young.

Because we are made of stars.

Dear Adult,

Please remember in the English dictionary and common parlance, dark and black are mostly described as bad, please don't forget that when teaching me.

The oppression of indigenous cultures is why there is adultification

Please don't forget that

It's not my fault

It's not your fault,

but you can change my life experience.

Please check out the history for each of these cultures:

The indigenous history of Africa

The indigenous history of the Caribbean

The indigenous history of America

The indigenous history or Brazil

The indigenous history of Australia

The indigenous history of Canada

The indigenous history of New Zealand

The history of dark-skinned people in Asia and the middle east

In fact:

Check out the indigenous people of every land in the world.

Everyone can be both good and bad sometimes.

Please don't pigeonhole

me into tropes like stereotypes

Every race has good and badly behaved people

That means I am not bad if I do something
seen as wrong –

I am human

please allow me to make mistakes and
explore

without labelling me as

the bad one.

Dear Adult,

Please remember

I was born like a blank sheet of paper to be written on.

Through my DNA I have infinite and spectacular possibilities.

With adult guidance, I can be molded into something greater than those who came before

epigenetics can shape my future

I am a child

I am new to the world

I am just experiencing life.

It may take many reminders for me to learn a behaviour you want to teach me

Please kindly teach me

If I do something wrong,

please don't repeatedly nag me

or look at me with an angry face
or tone, especially if I am in
nursery or primary school or
secondary school

That just confuses me and
inhibits my thinking

If I stole something, ...

it was because I wanted it, it excited me,

it does not make me and my racial group are more likely to steal things

Do teach me right from wrong

This book is for me,

for you and

everyone.

Signs of Adultification

- Disproportionate hostility
- A black child singled out and no one stands up for them
- A normalized pacified racism,
- Saying racism is complex and confusing and dismissed, when its simple, it is about being unfair

Adultification can appear when

Playing a video with all but one black character and the black character is inappropriate for a child's mind

allowing an SEN child to say something racist and not addressing it thoroughly

not regularly reading up on critical race theory written by scholars and not having done any recent anti-black racism training

Playing tunes by musicians who demonstrate colourism and shadism

Letting tunes with the N-word play publicly in a gym, in a yoga studio, on a playlist, in a party, in a theatre, a casual word between friends, letting it go, when you should say NO!

Being surprised about racism, when, racism is entrenched in society it's in nice people, please acknowledge and be a force for change.

Where is it?

Please remember racism can appear in the news, radio discussions,

in academic books, in the structure of modern education,

sometimes, it is indirect, mostly it is there like a bad odor unseen but sensed - it needs challenging.

Checking In

When you see a black child, what do you think?

If a negative thought, or fetish thought, or superior thought or condescending thought automatically appears, please work on this.

How?

By reading critical race theory, read at least 10 books.

Go on courses, be part of a multiracial community. Or even have anti-racism therapy.

What do you see?

When you see a white child what do you think?

Is that different to what you think about a black or Asian child?

If it is different, please do the work, to see us all as equally beautiful human beings

What do you think?

If a white child complains about a black child,

do you automatically assume the black child is bad, before checking.

If you do,

please do the work to learn about critical race theory and how it affects us all.

Please be bothered!

Please do not pigeonhole me into racial tropes

I am an individual,

the same way you are an individual

Black in the English dictionary is

Mostly negative

Dark in the English dictionary is

Mostly negative

Words like

niggardly and niggling

can be

used as a sly form of racism posturing

Be aware if you do this.

Language and History

Mostly, in historic and recent literature black is written as bad.

I am not bad.

Black for black people is a title given to describe the beautiful melanin pigment that enhances my life and is the colour of my great wonderful ancestors.

I am their legacy.

I will live long and strong

Adultification evidence can be,

an adult

- being heavy handed with a black child,
- having negative internal dialogues about black children
- Not checking that a black child has fully understood a task
- Not doing one-to-one with a black child when they do not understand
- Dismissing when a black child had behaviour issues and is SEN and not following up on their care
- Skipping over a black child but being attentive to other children

Evidence that I could be struggling

- Looking confused
- Being short sighted
- Always being quiet
- Showing anxiety
- Constant lateness
- Often disengaged
- Defensiveness
- Being told I have an attitude
- Staring
- Disorganized
- Truancy

Evidence that I could be adultified

- Low expectation
- Not knowing my needs
- Not nurturing my interests
- Not knowing my interest
- Presuming I am always wrong
- Not considering if I am SEN
- Not being of the same culture
- Being written off

Adultification can be ...

Thinking I am mature

because I am

clever,

tall or
broad or

in puberty

But I am still a child

Polite note to parents:

If you think your child is adultified.

Talk to your school

Get support

Question to adults:

How often should an adult be patient with a black child to prevent adultification?

Every time!

How can my child stand up for his or herself

Have this topic mentioned at the start of each term as part of INSET, with a CPD. Avoid crisis management.

The children will appreciate this.

What can my child do?

It's not their responsibility to solve this, but this example script can help in the right situation. This can be changed to your preferred wording.

Child: Excuse me Miss / Sir,

I say this with respect to you, I am not comfortable with what just happened, please take a moment to see if this is an example of adultification. Please speak with your line manager and my parents about this. I hope you are not offended by my reflection and assertion.

Thank you.

This script sounds like an adult speaking! Through adultification, the adult role is pressed onto a child.

Definition of a child:

The most precious person in a parent's life

The next generation of greatness and to be nurtured with care, wisdom and genius adults (or the next best version.)

Dear Carer,

Just because I do not articular like Piers, does not mean I am not as intelligent, I just come from a different background, that's all

Dear World,

I will present my child in a way so to celebrate their cultural grace; I am aware some styling may not celebrate cultural awareness.

Some black children are SEN. SEN children are more vulnerable

Pledge

As a care giver, I will do my utmost to ensure children in my care are assessed as soon as possible for any neurodivergent if suspected.

If there is any doubt a child in my care might be SEND, I will pursue until I have the right diagnosis so they can be supported.

I will check to see the support my child is receiving is effective and not performative

As an adult I pledge to

to stand for the children in my care

As a parent I pledge to:

Be responsible for my child and know at every stage on a daily basis, how my child is progressing in school

As a parent, I pledge to:

Know my child, through

Listening

Reading

Drawing

Problem solving

And Investing my time to know them

As a parent I pledge to:

> take my child on mind enhancing experiences, as much as I can afford, like museums, art galleries, the parks, hikes, countryside trips, fishing, sailing, playing chess, spiritual engagements, concerts, learning a musical instrument

And not just

> Leave my child alone for extended periods to use a tablet, a PC, a games console, a mobile phone, television or to indulge regularly in junk food

I pledge to listen to my child

As a parent I pledge to:

Find out as soon as possible if my child is SEND and to take supportive action if that is the case.

Some famous SEN people

Simone Biles -   has ADHD

Solange Knowles -   had ADHD

Harry Belafonte -   has Dyslexia

Danny Glover –   has Dyslexia

Magic Johnson –   has Dyslexia

Mohammed Ali –   has Dyslexia

-

How parents can help	How schools can help
Listen Research Talk to the school	Listen Research Invest Talk to parents

As a black child:

I don't like being disproportionately punished

I don't like being labelled the bad one

I know I do require fair consequences,

when I do things that adults disapprove of, like risky things.

As a black child:

Please block colonized teaching

Help me to decolonize my mind
without harming me in the process

As an educator I pledge to:

Keep my skills to a high level so I can effectively and holistically address decolonization by looking at myself first, before looking at anyone else

If my family were racist,

>on some level I may not be suitable to teach

>until

I have done the work,

>this includes:

reading anti-racism books,

taking regular effective anti-racism training,

work in a diverse community,

be in communication with woke adults,

even written extensively explaining how to defeat racist mentalities and   to not be

>a closet racist

Anti-Adultification Child Charter

To be heard

To wear a cardigan for warmth if my body is genetically sensitive to cold

To be treated with childhood respect

To be seen as good

To have had adjustments for cultural differences

To learn about my indigenous cultures

To have alternative technology

To be provided with high quality healthy food aligned with my ancestry

To be seen as an individual

To be allowed to explore when learning

Imagine

Imagine the anti-racism machine:

Takes every interaction, feeds it into an A.I. database, which checked for hostility, prejudice and bias.

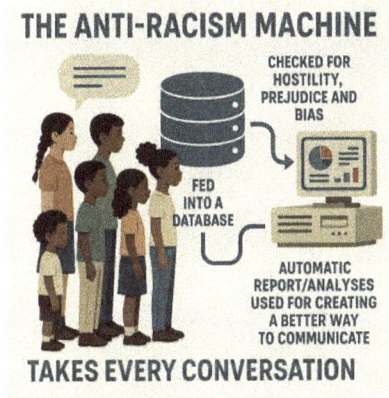

THE ANTI-RACISM MACHINE

CHECKED FOR HOSTILITY, PREJUDICE AND BIAS

FED INTO A DATABASE

AUTOMATIC REPORT/ANALYSES USED FOR CREATING A BETTER WAY TO COMMUNICATE

TAKES EVERY CONVERSATION

It analyses this and uses it for creating a better way to communicate with children

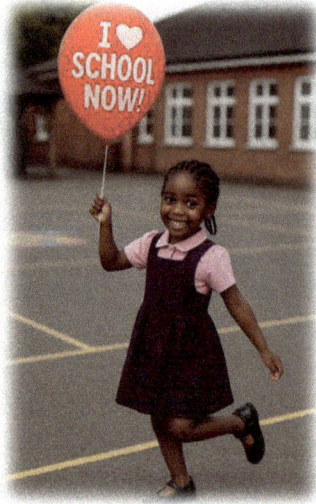

Quick Recap

1. What is adultification?

Treating black and brown children with a raised level of seriousness, which can result in them being more severely punished and labelled as bad.

2. How can it be identified?

In statistics black and brown children tend to be more penalized than white children when doing similar growing up offences.

3. What if I am a witness and it is not me carrying out the adultification?

If it is safe, intervene either immediately or later. Do not let the child suffer in silence.

4. What can I do if I am the perpetrator?

Read books on critical race theory. Do yearly unconscious bias testing. Have group therapy if the feelings are engrained. Self-assess if you are a suitable educator, TA, counsellor, head teacher, etc.

This book gives an outline of the experience of adultification.

It is recommended that, as well as discussing the issues raised in this book, follow-up activities are created by you to see how else to combat adultification in your own communities.

Thank you for reading this

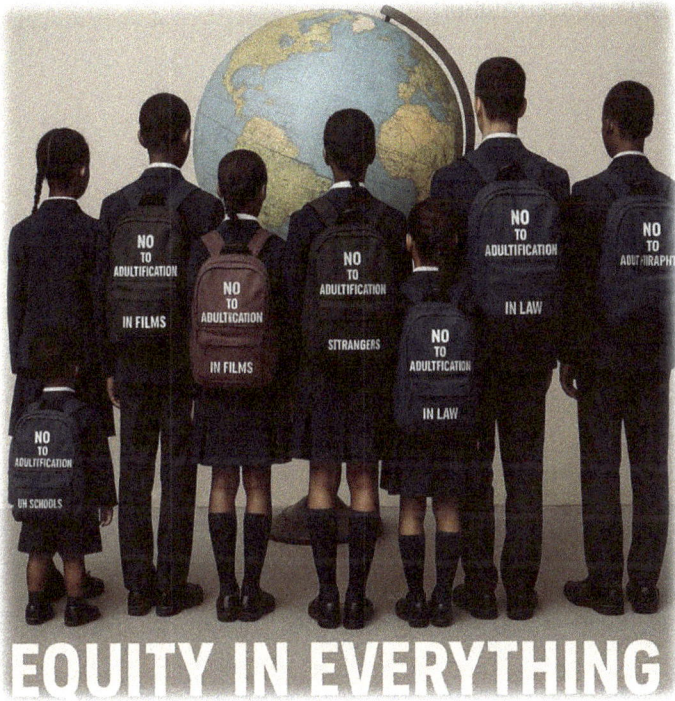

Together building a better world

Further Reading

Brit(ish): On Race, Identity and Belonging Paperback 2018

by Afua Hirsch (Author)

How Europe Underdeveloped Africa Paperback. 2018 by Walter

Rodney (Author),

The New Age of Empire: How Racism and Colonialism Still Rule the

World 2022 by Kehinde Andrews

The Fateful Triangle: Race, Ethnicity, Nation: 19 (The W. E. B. Du

Bois Lectures) Paperback 2021 b Stuart Hall